RACE CAR LEGENDS

The Allisons

Mario Andretti

Dale Earnhardt

A. J. Foyt

Richard Petty

The Unsers

CHELSEA HOUSE PUBLISHERS

RACE CAR LEGENDS

THE UNSERS

Karen Bentley

CHELSEA HOUSE PUBLISHERS

New York   Philadelphia

Acknowledgments

Thanks to Owen Snyder, team manager at Galles Racing International in Albuquerque, and Bobby Unser, race-car driver extraordinaire, for all their help in making this book.   —K.B.

Produced by Daniel Bial and Associates
New York, New York

Picture research by Alan Gottlieb
Cover illustration by Neil Maclaclan

First Printing

1 3 5 7 9 8 6 4 2

Library of Congress Cataloging-in-Publication Data

Bentley, Karen.
        The Unsers / Karen Bentley.
            p.   cm. — (Race car legends)
        Includes bibliographical references and index.
        Summary   Describes the lives and careers of the Unser family of
    automobile racing drivers, their rivalries with the Andretti family, and their
    victories at such major competitions as the Indianapolis 500.
        ISBN 0-7910-3186-1 (hc). — ISBN 0-7910-3187-X (pbk.)
        1. Unser, Al, Sr.—Juvenile literature.   2. Unser, Al, Jr.—Juvenile liter-
    ature.   3. Automobile racing drivers—United States—Biography—Juvenile
    literature.
        [1. Unser, Al, Sr.   2. Unser, Al, Jr.   3. Automobile racing drivers.]
    I. Title.   II. Series   95-18676
    GV1032.U56B45   1996   CIP
    796.7′2′0922 B—dc20   AC

CONTENTS

THE DRIVE TO WIN

Whaat's the most popular spectator sport in the United States? It's not baseball, football, basketball, or even horse racing. America's favorite sport is automobile racing.

To the outsider, it looks simple. You get in your car, keep the accelerator depressed as you hurtle around the track, expect your crew to keep the car in perfect condition, and try not to go deaf as you weave your machine through traffic toward the checkered flag. But in actuality, it's not at all easy. Just as baseball isn't simply a matter of hitting the ball, so racing is full of subtleties.

What does it take to be a world-class race car driver? The more you know about the lives of the greats, the more it becomes clear that each successful driver is an extraordinary athlete gifted with unusual vision, coordination, and the will to win. The concentration necessary to send a car speeding around a track at 200 miles per hour for hour after hour, when a momentary lapse can cause instant death for him and any unfortunate driver near him, is phenomenal. Any driver worth his salt must be strong, self-confident, resilient, and willing to take risks in order to have an opportunity to win.

In addition, the top drivers have to be good businessmen and know how to put together a winning team. They have to find sponsors to put them in competitive cars. They rely on a pit crew to make sure that their car is always in peak performance condition. And they have to be mentally prepared each race day to take into consideration a host of factors: weather, the other racers, the condition of the track, and how their car is responding on that day. Without everything right, a driver won't stand a chance of winning.

All the drivers in the Race Car Legends series grew up around race cars. The fathers of Richard Petty and Dale Earnhardt were very successful race car drivers themselves. A. J. Foyt's father was a part-time racer and a full-time mechanic; the Allisons and Unsers are an extended family of racers. Only Mario Andretti's father disapproved of his son's racing. Yet Mario and his twin brother Aldo devoted themselves to racing at a young age.

Despite the knowledge and connections a family can provide, few of the legendary racers portrayed in this series met with immediate success. They needed to prove themselves in sprint cars or midget cars before they were allowed to get behind the wheel of a contending stock car or a phenomenally expensive Indy car. They needed to be tested in the tough races on the hardscrabble tracks before they learned enough to handle the race situations at Daytona or the Brickyard. They needed to learn how to get the most out of whatever vehicle they were piloting, including knowing how to fix an engine in the wee hours of the night before a big race.

A driver also has to learn to face adversity, because crashes often take the lives of friends or relatives. Indeed, every driver has been lucky at one point or another to survive a scare or a bad accident. "We've had our tragedies, but what family hasn't?" remarked the mother of Al and Bobby Unser. "I don't blame racing. I love racing as our whole family has."

What each driver has proved is that success in this most grueling sport takes commitment. Walter Payton, the great football running back, and Paul Newman, star of many blockbuster movies, have both taken up racing—and proved they have some talent behind the wheel. Still, it's evident that neither has been able to provide the devotion it takes to be successful at the highest levels.

To be a great driver, racing has to be in your blood.

THE LEGEND CONTINUES: THE 1992 INDIANAPOLIS 500

The Indianapolis 500, the biggest event of race-car driving and one of the biggest sporting events in the world, was almost over. Only 11 laps of the 1992 race remained out of the 200 total laps in the 500-mile event. Half a million fans roared with excitement in the stands surrounding the Indianapolis Motor Speedway on that Memorial Day weekend, and millions more watched the race on television.

Michael Andretti, of the renowned Andretti racing family, shot his black-and-white Ford-powered race car into lap 189 of the asphalt Indy track. He had led for 163 of the first 189 laps and was comfortably ahead by several car lengths of Al Unser, Jr., in second place.

This race had already been the wildest Indy 500 in the race's 76-year history. Ten crashes had taken out 13 drivers, injuring three seriously. Only 12 drivers of the 33 cars that start-

Michael and Mario Andretti led at the start of the 1992 Indianapolis 500, but it was the Unser family that would make history on this day.

ed managed to finish the race at all on that cold, overcast day in Indianapolis, Indiana.

Al Unser, Jr., wanted terribly to beat Michael Andretti. One reason was the $1,244,184 first-place prize. Al, Jr., had never won the Indianapolis 500, and enormous pressure was on him to win. Although he was only 30 years old, this was his 10th Indy 500 attempt. His uncle Bobby and his father, Al Unser, Sr., had racked up seven Indy 500 victories between them: three for Uncle Bobby (in 1968, 1975, and 1981), and four for Al, Sr. (in 1970, 1971, 1978, and 1987). The Unsers had become the most successful Indy 500 racing family ever. Winning at the Indy 500 had become a family tradition.

The only other family that repeatedly competed at Indianapolis was the Andrettis: Mario, his two sons Michael and Jeff, and nephew John. After a combined 43 starts at the Indianapolis Motor Speedway, only Mario had ever won the checkered flag, in 1969.

The Andretti streak of misfortune at the Indy 500 continued in 1992. On lap 79, Mario Andretti hammered his car into the concrete outside wall, breaking toes on both feet. Jeff also smacked the outside wall, on lap 110, and broke bones in his legs, ankles, and feet. Both men needed to be taken to the hospital. Mario was back to racing in a matter of weeks. Jeff would require months of rehabilitation.

But Michael Andretti was running extremely well. Late in the race, he seemed to have the victory sewed up. Al Unser, Jr., was trying out a new car, and it had performed so poorly in practice—-the engine blew on the second day—that he didn't think he'd win anyway. Still, with 12 laps to go in the race, he had just whipped

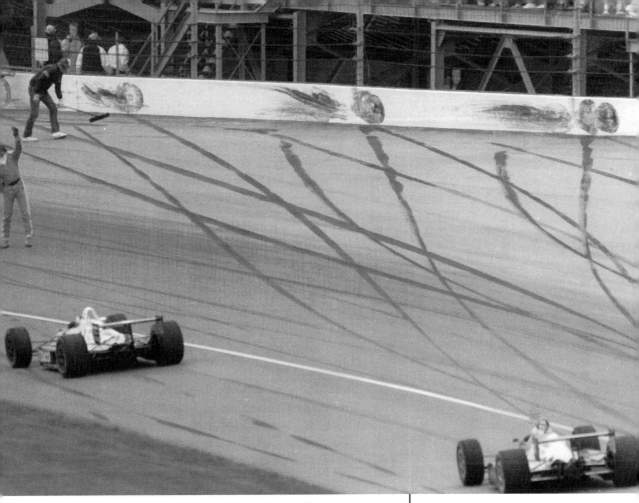

around 30-year-old Canadian Scott Goodyear's blue-and-silver Lola-Chevy (Lola chassis, Chevy engine) to move into second place.

Al Unser, Sr., the father of Al, Jr., drove his Lola-Buick up into fourth place. Although he set a record for the most laps led at the Indianapolis 500, Al, Sr., had come to the 1992 Indy 500 without a decent ride. He only got a chance to race when a rookie was injured in practice. He was racing very well for someone who was driving an unfamiliar car. But he seemed to pose no threat to Andretti, who had mopped up the field for most of the race.

The Indy cars were averaging 220 miles per hour on the straightaways and 200 miles per

Skid marks and tire impact markings on the wall of the first turn give evidence of the number of crashes during the 1992 Indy.

All Al Unser, Jr., had to do was hold off Scott Goodyear to win the big race.

hour on the corners. They were flying around the 2.5-mile oval track in about 45 seconds.

Al, Sr., and Bobby Unser had taught Al, Jr., well. Al, Sr., had a reputation as a patient driver who was very good in long races like the Indy

500: he paced himself and saved the car, not running it harder than he had to. Bobby Unser was an innovator in races and drove every lap like it was the last lap of the race. Al, Jr., drives hard when he needs to but paces himself.

Suddenly, 11 laps from the finish line, Michael Andretti's car slowed. A fuel pump drive belt had broken. In a split second the race was over for him. The fabled Andretti bad luck had struck again.

"It can't get much worse than this," Michael Andretti said after he bailed out of his broken half-million-dollar car. "This place is cruel, so cruel."

Al Unser, Jr., took the lead in his red, white, blue, and black Chevy after Andretti's car coasted to a stop at the side of the track.

"I felt for Mikey," he said. "But a second later, I had Scott Goodyear right up my tailpipe."

Goodyear (who is no relation to members of the tire company family) had started the race last but managed to move up to 20th after just eight laps. He'd expertly worked his way up to third place, then took second when Andretti was out of the race. That kind of maneuvering through traffic was extremely difficult in this Indy 500. Goodyear and the other drivers had to dodge debris from the almost constant wrecks that littered the track.

The unseasonably cold weather caused most of the carnage. Many wrecks happened soon after pit stops, when the drivers pull the cars off the track to refuel and get new tires. After each pit stop the cars' new, cold racing slicks, or tires, had to be carefully "scuffed" through a series of tight, wiggly maneuvers so that they would properly grip the track. But to do that, the drivers had to move slowly out of pit stops and take the time to warm up the tires.

The cars were set wrong for the race-day weather, too. In the final practice the Thursday before the race, the laps had been run in sunny, 80-degree temperatures. The mechanics had adjusted their cars for a hot, sticky track. Then the temperature dropped into the 50s on Sunday, race day. The conditions were so bad that one driver, Roberto Guerrero, spun into the wall on the second parade lap, before the race had even officially begun. Guerrero had set a track record in practice of four laps averaging 232.482 miles per hour, but on race day he inadequately warmed up his tires.

Al, Jr., started the race 12th. Like Goodyear, he nimbly picked his way through the traffic. He was 10th after 100 miles, fifth after 200, fourth after 300, and third after 400. "I was warming up my tires from the beginning of the race," Unser said. "I was extremely careful."

Goodyear and Al, Jr., drove furiously for the finish. On the last few laps of the race Goodyear tried again and again to pass. Unser's and Goodyear's cars seemed tied together by puppet strings. Al dove to the inside of the track around corners. Goodyear dove after him. Al zigged to the outside of the track on straightaways. Goodyear zagged after him.

Unser, the more experienced driver, was expertly using a lot of track to prevent Goodyear from getting behind him in his draft. If Goodyear had been able to get in Unser's tow, he might have been able to swing around Unser for the pass. "Experience is hard to get and hard to beat," remarked Owen Snyder, team manager at Galles

International Racing, which was behind Unser's 1992 Indy 500 run.

"I don't call what Al, Jr., did blocking; I call it using a lot of racetrack," Goodyear said diplomatically later. Deliberately blocking another car is illegal in Indy-car racing.

On the final turn before the checkered flag flashed down to signal the end of the race, Unser's car slid dangerously. He backed off the throttle—the other choice was to spin into the concrete wall outside the track. Goodyear saw his chance and tried to slip around Unser on the inside.

Unser fought him off. "I tried to make the race car as wide as I could. I was talking to it, saying, 'Come on. Let's go!'" he said.

Racing at over 220 miles per hour on the final straightaway, Unser managed to block Goodyear until the last 100 yards of the race. Then, in a

The Unser family history at the Indianapolis 500 goes back to 1929, when (left to right) Jerry, Louis, and Joe Unser were preparing to enter the race. Unfortunately, Joe was killed while testing this car prior to the big day.

burst of speed, Goodyear swept around Unser's car on the inside.

"He got a run on me like you wouldn't believe. He gave me one heckuva scare that he was going to take it away then," Al, Jr., said. "I moved over a little bit to block but finally decided to move straight on, and that the best man was going to win. Scott was right under my exhaust."

Al, Jr., blazed across the finish line .043 of a second—about half a car length—ahead of Scott Goodyear to win the closest Indy 500 ever.

Al's average speed was slow for an Indy 500—134.479 miles per hour. The average speed had been reduced by yellow caution flags, when the drivers must slow down while debris from accidents is cleared from the track.

"Very seldom does the fastest car win the race in the Indy 500. Al, Jr.'s not always the fastest guy, but at the end of the race you look, and there he is. He never gives up—that's the thing that makes him special," said Owen Snyder.

"What my father has instilled in me is that only one lap is what you want to lead, and that's the last lap," Al, Jr., said.

Al, Sr., was the only other driver to complete the 200 laps of the 1992 Indy 500, placing third. With Al, Jr.'s win, they became the first father-son winning combination at the Indy 500.

When his son took the checkered flag, the usually unemotional Al, Sr., broke down. "To love something as much as I love racing," he said, "and then to have your son come along and win here is the greatest feeling there is."

"Indy means life to me. I've been trying to do this since I was a little boy. This is just a dream come true," Al, Jr., said simply.

After the race he returned to his motor home, parked just outside the track. A sign had been painted in yellow on the windshield, proclaiming, "There is a God!"

The sign seemed to mean that Unser had been watched over in the race, unlike the hapless Andrettis. Or maybe it meant that he had joined the pantheon of race-car gods who have won at Indianapolis.

"BOBBY DROVE HARD, ALL THE TIME"

The famous Unser racing family began their association with cars around the turn of the century. Then, Louis Unser, grandfather of Bobby and Al, Sr., began to make his living as a mechanic in Colorado Springs, Colorado.

Louis's three sons—Louis, Jr., Jerry, and Joe—made a name for themselves by riding two motorcycles and a sidecar to the top of Colorado's Pike's Peak in the 1920s. This mountain is 14,110 feet high and stands out at the edge of the Great Plains as a portent of the Rockie Mountains nearby. Pike's Peak has always been considered a challenge to hike up, and for many years no one thought to try to drive up it. For one thing, the road stopped three quarters of the way to the top.

In the first race up Pike's Peak about 40 drivers competed with the Unsers. All the others turned back. The Unsers won by default.

Bobby Unser sits behind the wheel of the car that won him his first Pike's Peak victory.

Soon after the Unsers drove up Pike's Peak through the rocks and brush, Spencer Penrose, a local philanthropist, built the rest of the road and began to sponsor a yearly race up the mountain. That race up Pike's Peak, sometimes called Unsers' Peak, became a proving ground for Unser drivers.

Jerry Unser, the father of Bobby and Al, Sr., always built and worked on the cars he drove. He was also a pilot, doing barnstorming shows— flying across the country and performing stunts, mostly in rural areas. Then he lost his license for souping up the engines of his airplanes in violation of federal regulations. Eventually he became a movie stunt driver.

Jerry and his third wife, Mary, had four sons: twins Jerry, Jr., and Louie, Bobby (15 months younger), and Al (five years younger than Bobby). Jerry moved his family from Colorado Springs to Albuquerque, New Mexico, in 1936 and opened a garage and filling station on Route 66. "Daddy could fix things nobody else could," Bobby remarked.

All four Unser boys quickly graduated from riding wild burros they caught on the mesa outside Albuquerque to Model A Fords. When Bobby Unser was just eight years old, he was already driving his Model A on the dirt mesa roads near his home.

By the time Jerry and Louie were 16 years old and Bobby was 15, they had graduated to driving race cars. They established themselves as a force on the local short tracks across New Mexico, Colorado, and Arizona.

The Unsers were aggressive competitors in and out of race cars. "Several times we had to back out of a racetrack because we were fighting,"

The Unser boys smile in an early family photo.

Louie admitted. "A couple of times we had to leave before the police arrived."

Jerry, Jr., was the first Unser to become a national champion: United States Auto Club (USAC) stock car champion in 1957. "He was the first really big thing to come out of Albuquerque," said Louie, who made a career on the West Coast building race-car engines. In 1958, Jerry was also the first Unser to make it to the Indy 500. But in 1959, Jerry crashed on the first day of practice there and was badly burned. "He had what they call third-degree burns," said Louie. "But really they don't have a number to describe how bad he was burned over his back and legs and kidneys."

Although race-car driving will always be an extremely dangerous sport, today's Indy cars are safer. The wheels fall off so that cars now skid down the track instead of flipping. Methanol is used as fuel instead of gasoline because methanol ignites less quickly, reducing the risk of fire. (The only problem with methanol fuel is that the dim blue flames of a methanol fire are hard to see—sometimes a driver is invisibly on fire.) In a fire, the fire-resistant suits drivers wear give them about 30 seconds of protection.

Jerry died 17 days later of pneumonia and kidney failure. With today's modern medicine, he would have stood a better chance. In 1959, kidney dialysis machines, which help a person survive kidney failure, were still primitive.

In those days, deaths at the track were common—some say even half of all drivers died due to accidents. Jerry's death, although a personal tragedy for the Unsers, didn't affect their racing style. He had taken risks they all did.

After Jerry's death, Bobby Unser, who along with his younger brother Al would make race-car history, emerged as the Unser to beat in racing. Bobby began his career racing stock cars in New Mexico at age 15. At age 16, he won the Southwest Modified Stock Car Championship.

Sometimes Bobby's early victories were under harrowing circumstances. At Speedway Park in Albuquerque in 1951, Bobby was running third in a stock-car race behind older, more experienced drivers. Then the front runner's car burst into a spectacular gasoline fire that lit up the entire track. Bobby took the lead and won.

When he was 17, and still not old enough to hold a competition license, Bobby drove his father's car in the annual Pan-American Road Race, from Tuxtla Gutierrez at the south end of Mexico to Juarez in the north. His father started the race and then changed places with under-age Bobby. "Daddy and I could change seats while still on the move," Bobby said.

Later that same year, 1951, Bobby was at Pike's Peak, determined to make a name for himself at the race. "My uncle Louie told me that if I came up to Pike's Peak for practice, he would let me drive his car on roads off the mountain," Bobby said. But his uncle ran the car himself every day. "I became kind of bitter," Bobby commented.

Discouraged and completely out of money, he and a friend left for home. The only way they could get there with no money was to siphon gas from vehicles they found along the way. Siphoning gas was an art: not every tank the two friends tried was full, and so they usually had to raid several tanks to fill up their own. "In those days it would have been nothing for some guy to poke

a gun out the window of his house and shoot you," Bobby said.

Just as Bobby and his friend pulled into Pueblo, Colorado, they saw a race car being towed the other way. They followed the car to the track in Pueblo. Once there, Bobby put on his racing jacket and told the officials he was a racing champion from New Mexico. That was sufficient to get himself and his friend free pit passes. Once they could approach the crews, Bobby found a car to drive in the race, despite the fact that he was still only 17 and underage. However, he had a fake birth certificate stating that he was 22, a year older than the legal age to drive in the race.

Bobby Unser drove most of the 1952 Mexican Road Race. "Daddy's on the right and I'm on the left," he said. "Daddy would drive around the first corner and then we'd switch."

Bobby on his way to his first Pike's Peak win in 1956. He would eventually win 13 Pike's Peak titles.

Bobby won at Pueblo. The two jubilant friends headed for home. They now had the princely sum of $80, enough for food, a motel, and gas (in those days gas cost about 15 or 20 cents a gallon).

It was still a while longer before the Unsers became the wealthy, famous family that they are today. In 1955, Bobby lived in a tiny house in the desert at the edge of Albuquerque. "We used to raise centipedes and black widows in that house," Bobby remembered. "When the sand would blow really bad, sometimes we would just open the doors and let it blow on through."

Bobby Unser would return to Pike's Peak. In 1955, Bobby's first year racing there, he placed fifth. Louie and Jerry placed third and fourth respectively, Louie in a car Bobby loaned him.

In the Pike's Peak race the next year, Bobby was driving the car he had loaned Louie the year before. The three Unser brothers were running against famous drivers Bob Finney and Slim Roberts, who were racing cars for Dick Frenzel's big-time operation out of Denver, Colorado. "I was definitely favored *not* to win," Bobby said.

That year, 1956, was when the Unsers began to change racing at Pike's Peak. The Jaguar engines in their cars were small compared to big-league V-8s run by Frenzel. But the Unser cars were lighter. Their Jaguar engines turned more revolutions per minute (rpm), and Jerry, Sr., had invented a special racing camshaft for them. Both improvements provided more power at higher speeds. The Unser cars' engines were also a bigger, more powerful 3.8-liter instead of the standard 3.5-liter engine.

Bobby Unser won the race. "That race was a storybook affair," he remarked. "That was the turnaround in my career. I became a famous person overnight."

He went on to win at Pike's Peak for six years in a row, from 1958 through 1963. In all but one race he set records. Finally, in 1986, he topped Uncle Louie's nine victories at the mountain. Bobby Unser now has a record 13 Pike's Peak titles.

"The Unser brothers raced at Pike's Peak to beat each other and most of all to beat Uncle Louis," Bobby said. "That was what got me into racing—not to win the Indianapolis 500 three times but to beat Uncle Louis."

Although he achieved his goal of beating Uncle Louis, Bobby Unser also won the Indy 500 three times: in 1968, 1975, and 1981. "To win at Indy is a function of not making any mistakes all day long," Bobby remarked. "You need a good game plan and good thinking—you have to be at a peak in your performance."

His first Indy 500 win, in 1968, was in record time against hard competition. Three turbine cars—cars with jet engines—were in the race. The turbine feature seemed to give these drivers a big advantage over the rest of the field.

One turbine-car driver was killed in practice before the race. Bobby Unser then battled the remaining three. His brother, Al, Sr., was also in the race. About halfway to the finish, Al's car lost a wheel and hit the wall. Al climbed to the top of the wall and waved to Bobby, signaling that he was okay.

Bobby had managed to lead over half of that Indy 500, but then he broke a gearshift lever. From then on he had only one gear—fourth. (After a stop a car usually moves through first, second, and third gears to work up speed.) "It took a long time to get that sucker going after pit stops," Bobby remarked. The broken lever caused him to lose about a lap every time he pitted.

But the turbine cars were also having problems. The team's sponsor, an oil company, was running them on gasoline instead of jet fuel. The gasoline was an oil-company product, and having the race cars run on it was good publicity.

"The drivers had to back out the power of their engines to bring down the temperature of the gasoline fuel," Bobby said. "Now they were playing in my playground."

Bobby Unser at the Riverside Grand Prix in 1958.

At the dash to the finish after the last pit stop, Joe Leonard was leading in his turbine. Art Pollard, driving another turbine, blocked Unser, keeping him back in second.

Suddenly, with only about 15 laps to go, first Leonard's, then Pollard's car slowed to a stop. The cars' engine-fuel pumps had seized up. The reason was that gasoline is a poor lubricant, unlike jet fuel.

Unser had no other competition in the race. The 400,000 people in the stands rose to their

With 32.5 miles to go in the 1968 Indianapolis 500, Joe Leonard's turbine car rolls to a halt. Bobby Unser whips past to win the checkered flag.

feet, cheering. He coasted to his first Indianapolis victory.

Success didn't come without a price, though. In a 1973 Indy-car race at Phoenix, Unser suffered his worst and most spectacular wreck ever. "I was leading the race," he said, "and passing Gary Bettenhausen, who was a lap down. He pushed me into the wall. That first hit wasn't so bad. But my car spun and hit another wall. The car disintegrated."

In the past 20 years the safety features added to Indy cars make such a complete wipeout less likely. An Indy car must weigh at least 1,550 pounds, whereas the Formula 1 cars, a fast European kind of race car, weigh only 1,150 pounds. Most of the extra Indy-car weight are safety features, such as reinforcement around the driver.

"That was such a bad-looking wreck, even the firemen wouldn't come near it—they were afraid it was going to explode," Bobby continued. "But I needed help. I couldn't get out of the car because I was broken up all over. My shoulder was broken, both feet, every one of my ribs on both sides."

Bobby's brother Al was in the same race. The brothers often raced against each other in the same races, on different teams, and it was their policy not to stop when the other crashed. But this time Al stopped. "The first guy who got to me was my brother," Bobby said. Al pulled Bobby out of the car, taking himself out of the race.

"Al went in the helicopter with me," Bobby said. "But at the hospital no doctors were waiting. They put me in a holding room. I was hurting so bad, it was unbelievable. I'd wake up, then go unconscious again. Finally Al grabbed a doctor walking down the hall by the shirt and just dragged him into the room."

Bobby was taken to the X-ray room. The technicians moved the machine above Bobby's eyes to begin total-body X-rays. Suddenly one of the machine's rubber cables caught fire, and hot rubber dripped toward his face. The technicians took off running. But because of his severe injuries, Bobby couldn't move.

Al was leaning up against the wall outside the room. When he saw the technicians run out, he hurried inside, pushed the machine away from Bobby's face, and wheeled his brother back into the hallway.

"For a couple of days they didn't know if I was going to make it or not," Bobby said. "My neck was swollen so badly, it was pinching off the blood running up and down the jugular vein." He never did get X-rays. "I didn't know my feet were broken until I tried to walk on them." His broken bones finally mended, although crookedly, without treatment.

Serious wrecks are common for a race-car driver, especially one with Bobby Unser's racing style. He developed a reputation as an uncompromisingly aggressive driver.

"He drove hard, all the time," said Owen Snyder of Galles International Racing.

"That pretty much describes my central philosophy," Bobby agreed.

Unser always pushed himself and his team almost to the breaking point. "Total commitment is what a race-car driver needs more than good eyesight or raw talent," he said. "And concentration: Not many drivers can concentrate all the way through a race, although they think they can."

Bobby Unser also worked on his cars. Sometimes these experiments resulted in mechanical or tactical failure. But he probably won more races by always searching for more speed or a greater technical advantage.

The tactic paid off in the 1968 Indy 500. Bobby had bought and helped innovate a new turbocharged engine for his first Indy win instead of going with a safer, older Ford engine.

In 1982, at the age of 48, Bobby Unser retired from driving Indy cars. He has been married four times and has four children: Bobby, Jr., Cindy, Robby, and Jeri. He currently works as a sportscaster for ABC Sports Television.

His retirement from Indy cars was by no means the end of his driving career. In 1993 he set a new land-speed record of 223.709 miles per hour in a D gas-modified roadster, a class of cars run in the famous international road race at Bonneville Salt Flats in Utah. That same year he won the Fastmasters invitational race for drivers over 50, driving identical Jaguar XJ 220s, and took home $115,000. In 1994, he was inducted into the International Motorsports Hall of Fame.

His Fastmasters victory was never much in doubt: Unser led the entire 12-lap race. He had the second-fastest average time in practice laps and began the race in the front row, on the outside. That was a good position, but not as good as the inside front-row position George Folmer had qualified for on the narrow track.

"Somebody will have to give on that first turn," Bobby commented.

"I guarantee you, Bobby ain't givin' up nothin'," the sportscaster predicted correctly.

3
AL, SR.:
"HE WAS FAST
RIGHT OFF THE BAT"

For me to want or even think about being better than my father would be presumptuous. If I could stay one step behind my father throughout my entire life, then I would be a successful person," Al, Jr., remarked. "I've said this as a kid, and I still mean it today: My dad is one of the greatest racing drivers who ever lived, and his record shows it."

Al Unser, Sr., won the Indianapolis 500 four times: in 1970, 1971, 1978, and 1987. With four wins, he is tied with Rick Mears and A. J. Foyt for the most wins in the Indy 500. He is also the fourth and last driver to win two consecutive Indy 500s (the others were Wilbur Shaw, 1939–40; Mauri Rose, 1947–48; and Bill Vukovich, 1953–54).

Al, Sr., started racing at age 17. "He was fast right off the bat," said his older brother Bobby. Al won the first race he ever entered, at Speed-

Al Unser, Sr., worked at his father's garage after he left school. "He paid me $7 a week. And I bought a car and I bought all my clothes after that."

At Sacramento in 1965, Al (#40) has a lead over brother Bobby (#88), while Jud Larson (#10) and A. J. Foyt (#1) are close behind.

way Park in Albuquerque, in a stock car built by his father and Bobby. Soon he had a string of victories.

Other drivers started picking on him. "Grownups don't like kids to outrun them," Bobby remarked. "So I started racing with Al. He and I would take turns who was going to win each race. We could dictate, because we were far faster than anyone else. If anyone gave us trouble after the race, we'd fight them. We put out a message: Don't screw with the Unsers.

"Al and I have always gone down the same roads," Bobby added. "Not lying, not stealing, not cheating—we got the same things from our parents." Nevertheless, the two Unser brothers have very different personalities: Bobby's way with words has resulted in a job as an ABC sportscaster, whereas the reticence of Al, Sr., is legendary.

Al won his first Pike's Peak race in 1964, setting a new course record and breaking Bobby's six-race winning streak. The Pike's Peak races were the real contest between Al and Bobby. "He'd build his car over on one side of the street and I'd build mine on the other," said Bobby. "I couldn't go over to see his, and he couldn't come over to see mine. So we'd go to the racetrack and see who had done his best thinking and best homework.

"It would get tense between me and Al about who would win, but it never stayed. We were able to separate business and family—we never really got in a fight. We never let it come down to anything other than racing. Even though he's my brother, we can't be brothers on the racetrack. It took a lot of work and practice to keep it that way. We never talked about racing—not about secret things. He would never try to pump me for secrets and I would never try to pump him."

The next step for an Unser after a Pike's Peak win was to make a run at Indianapolis. "When I was a kid, every year when the Indianapolis was run, I was glued to the radio, and I said that someday I would be there," Al said. His first run at the Indy 500, in 1965, was in a car owned by A. J. Foyt. Al placed ninth, not bad considering he had started in the last row.

The more Al learned about Indy, the better he did. In 1966, Unser was running third when he wrecked his car. The following year, he came in second, behind Foyt.

Bobby won the 1968 race. "I was happy for him, but jealous of him. You want your brother to do good, but I guess you're not human if you don't want to do better. We both wanted to be the first Unser to win Indy and he got there first."

Al's car was hot in 1969, and he was the favorite to win. But the day before qualifying began, Al broke his leg while driving a motorcycle in the parking lot. "Missing Indianapolis that year was the biggest disappointment in my life. I'd not only let myself down, but everyone who'd worked on the car."

He didn't have long to wait to get back to winning. Al won five races that year after the cast came off. And in 1970, he claimed the pole position at Indianapolis. Johnny Rutherford and A. J. Foyt were right beside him at the start of the race, but Unser quickly pulled away.

At mile 120, Lloyd Ruby took the lead. Ten laps later, oil spurted into his exhaust pipe; his car became a flaming torch, and he had to retire. Unser regained the lead and never relinquished it. After 200 miles, he came up on A. J. Foyt, who was in second place. Instead of passing, Unser slipped his blue-and-gold P. J. Colt–Ford behind Foyt's car; for the next 200 miles Foyt raced all out and Unser drafted behind him. Foyt suffered a broken gear box in avoiding a crash and finished tenth. Unser and his Johnny Lightning "500" Special cruised on to win by 32 seconds over his nearest competitor. He became the first pole sitter to win the race since 1963.

The 1970 race was the first to feature a total purse of over one million dollars. Unser also set a record with his winner's share of over $250,000.

In 1970, Al had about as good a year as any racer has ever had. He won his first Indianapolis 500. He also became the only person ever to win racing's Triple Crown, the three 500-mile races then on the Indy-car circuit: Indy, Ontario, and Pocono. In total, he won 10 of 18 races (which tied a record set by A. J. Foyt) and the USAC national championship.

"When it came to those long races, like the 500s, Al, Sr., was going to be there," one racing expert said.

The 1971 Indy saw Unser start in third position. The first, second, and fourth cars were all McLaren M-16s, a new car designed by Bruce McLaren that featured a spoiler wing in back

Al Unser, Sr., won his third Indy 500 in 1978. Besides his total four victories, Al, Sr., also finished second three times. Bobby and Al, Jr., have finished second once each.

and two small ones in front. Unser commented before the race, "Our only hope of winning is to put pressure on these M-16s and hope they won't hold up."

Mark Donahue, in one of the M-16s, blazed out to a 30-second lead. He ran his 66th lap at 174.91 mph—six miles an hour faster than any one had previously run a lap in traffic. On the next lap his car broke down. "When I saw Donahue was out," Unser said, "my heart did an extra lurch because I knew everyone else had a chance."

The only other trouble Unser had came in the 113th lap when David Hobbs and Rick Muther got tangled up on the back stretch. "I came out of the fourth turn and saw them banging around, debris flying. I started to lock up my brakes. Trouble was, I couldn't see any place to go, so I decided to try the low route. If one of those cars had come sliding down across the track, I would have been history."

Al Unser became history anyway. He was the fourth person ever to win back-to-back Indy 500s.

In 1972, Unser had to settle for second behind Mark Donahue at the Indianapolis 500. Jerry Grant originally finished in front of Unser, but he was penalized 10 places for taking gas from Bobby's pit when his own tanks ran dry. If Unser seemed lucky to be awarded second place, that luck soon ran out. He didn't win another race all year. He didn't win again at the Indianapolis 500 until 1978, when he beat Tom Sneva.

Each year, between March and October, Indy cars compete in 16 races in the United States, Canada, and Australia. The races are sanctioned by the Championship Auto Racing Teams (CART) organization. CART is to Indy car racing what the National Football League, the NFL, is to pro football. CART sets the Indy-car racing rules.

In 1985, Al, Sr., won the CART/PPG Cup Championship by one point, 151 to 150, over Al, Jr., with 11 top-10 finishes in 14 races. It was the closest championship battle in Indy-car history and the first and only time a father and son finished one-two in the championship point standings. (Indy car drivers are awarded points for each race: 20 for first place and 16 for second. The fastest qualifier—the driver with the fastest average speed in four laps driven before the race—gets a point, and so does the driver who led for the most laps in the race. The season's champion gets over $1 million.)

Al, Sr., had driven against his son as hard as he could that year. "It's the same way I treated my brother Bobby when we were racing together," Al, Sr., said. "But that feeling was a lot easier to handle than this one."

As Memorial Day of 1987 approached, Al found himself without a good ride for the Indy 500, despite his distinguished record as a driver.

"I had never been at Indianapolis without a ride," Al said in 1987. "It was a very lonely, empty feeling." He finally found one with Roger Penske's team when Danny Ongais crashed in the first week of practice. Penske provided a leftover Ford March that he had been displaying at auto shows. Al was almost completely unfamiliar with the car, but he managed to qualify for the 20th position.

The 1987 Indy 500 started off poorly for Al. In the first turn of the race, a driver spun into the wall, barely missing him. Then Al stalled out leaving the first pit stop, an unusual mistake for him. "Come on, Al! Pay attention to what you're supposed to be doing!" he told himself.

Slowly but surely moving forward, Al was driving in the top 10 by lap 50 and in the top five by lap 60. Finally he was third, behind Mario Andretti and Roberto Guerrero. "There was no way I could run with Mario," Al said—until Mario's engine quit 60 miles from the finish.

Guerrero took the lead, but he was having problems too. An overheated clutch kept slipping. He and Al fought to the checkered flag. When the flag flashed down, Al had won his fourth Indy 500 by 4.5 seconds.

"The Speedway has been good to me, you know," Al commented. In 1991 he was inducted into the International Motorsports Hall of Fame of America.

In 1994, Al failed to drive fast enough in practice laps to qualify for the Indy 500. "It takes 100 percent to race one of these cars," Al, Sr., said. "I finally realized I wasn't producing like I should. I can't tell the mechanics what the car's doing, and I should be able to. If the car was perfect, maybe I could go out there and run." Al announced his retirement a few days before the race.

Ironically, after he retired, the quietest Unser found more time to play the race-car sponsorship game. When a company invests big money in a racing team, the drivers are often expected to show up at company meetings, shake hands with corporate vice presidents, make personal appearances—whatever will help company sales. Before, Al had always preferred driving, spending time at the family lodge in Chama, New Mexico (Al has been married twice and also has a daughter, Mary Linda), and avoiding idle conversation.

Sponsors are critical in the expensive sport of Indy-car racing. Each car costs about $600,000, and two cars are needed in case one breaks down. The driver and race team have to be paid. A huge tractor-trailer hauls the cars and serves as an on-site machine shop. A year of Indy-car racing easily runs into millions of dollars.

Five or 10 years ago, driving ability used to be all that mattered in racing. But in the high-technology age, racing has gotten so expensive that no one can afford to race without sponsors.

Al, Sr., announced his retirement from racing just days short of his 55th birthday. If he had raced at Indy, it would have been his 28th appearance.

But as a birthday present for him, Al, Jr., won the 1994 Indianapolis 500.

4

AL, JR.: NAPOLEON AT THE RACETRACK

I've always loved racing, says Al Unser, Jr. "I worked in a machine shop when I was 15 to get the money to buy my car. I never wanted to pursue anything else. I thought that if I could be halfway successful with racing, then I'd stay with it."

Today Al, Jr., is considered the top driver on the Indy-car circuit and one of the top five drivers in the world.

He began riding dirt bikes at the age of six. The next year his father gave him a minibike, and when he was nine, Al, Jr., started driving go-karts. "My dad would tell me if I made a mistake and how to correct it," Al, Jr., said. "But he never raised his voice at me about my driving."

"I wanted him to race," Al, Sr., said. "When we started in go-karts, it was me pushing it. I think I got more of a charge out of it than he did. We

In 1969, Al Unser, Sr., gave Al, Jr., his first minibike. Al, Jr., wasn't allowed to drive it for a week— because he had been grounded the night before for misbehaving.

used to go out every weekend and run the karts. That's how he got started. Everybody kept saying, 'He's going to be three times better than you.' And I always used to say that I hoped he was, but one step at a time. Al always progressed very rapidly, and he was good at racing."

Al, Jr., entered his first professional race, in the World of Outlaws series, when he was 16. He drove a sprint car: a small, dirt-track racer. "Racing sprint cars on the dirt taught me to hustle the race car and run wheel to wheel," he said. "The World of Outlaws series was a good place to learn because it was very aggressive racing." After he finished high school, Al, Jr., started racing on dirt tracks full time.

"I just couldn't believe that an 18-year-old could do what he could," Al, Sr., said about his son's performance in sprint cars.

Al, Jr.'s talent as a driver was clear from a very early age. But racing wasn't something he had to do as a living. Financial necessity wouldn't drive him the way it had his father and uncle. "One thing I had trouble with him doing is making sure he focused in," Al, Sr., remarked.

"Probably Al, Jr., had everything he ever wanted," said a friend of his. "At some point, though, he had to buckle down and say, 'Okay, I want to be a race-car driver and I'm going to work hard to do that.' And he did."

After sprint cars Al, Jr., moved up to Super Vees—race cars with Volkswagen engines. (Racing Super Vees used to be like playing triple-A baseball—these cars were the last stop before Indy cars, or the pros.)

When he was just 19, the Sports Car Club of America (SCCA) named Al, Jr., Rookie of the Year. In 1983 he won at Pike's Peak, setting a record

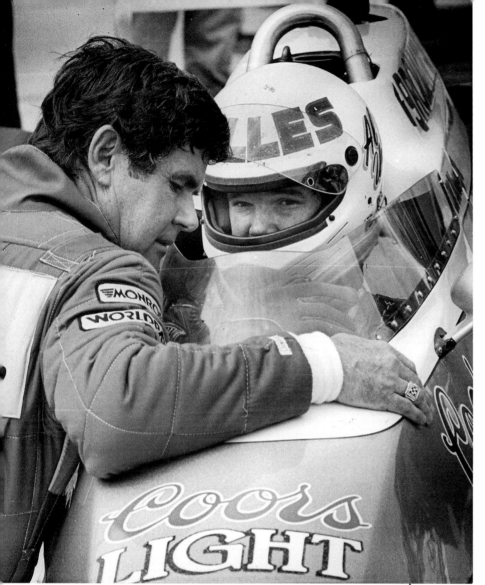

In 1983, Al, Jr., made his debut at the Indianapolis 500. Both father and son had laps at over 200 mph as they prepared for the race.

and ensuring that the family legend of winning there would continue.

At age 21, Al, Jr., was a rookie driver in the Indy 500 race. "For the first time I had butterflies in my stomach at a racetrack," he said.

Al, Jr., knew about his father's legendary wins at the Indy 500 mostly through hearsay. He was too young to be at Indianapolis for his father's first two wins there, in 1970 and 1971, and he missed the third in 1978 when his parents left him at home in Albuquerque after catching him ditching school.

"This is not a magical place," Al, Sr., reassured him. "It's just another racetrack, and if you treat it like that, you'll be all right." Al, Jr., became the youngest driver to pass the 200-mile-per-hour barrier at Indy, and he placed 10th in that race. In 1984 he won his first Indy-car victory at Portland International Raceway on Father's Day.

By 1986, he was the youngest International Race of Champions (IROC) winner, taking three of four races in the series. In IROC races, all drivers use identical cars, so that only the drivers' skill is tested.

In 1990, Unser won six CART races, tying the record for races won in a single season with Uncle Bobby (1979), Rick Mears (1981), Mario Andretti (1984), and Bobby Rahal (1986).

By winning four consecutive Indy-car races at Toronto, Michigan, Denver, and Vancouver in 1990, Al, Jr., established a CART record for victories in succession (four). He also became the first second-generation Indy-car champion in history, with 210 points, and the first Indy-car driver to break the 200-point record.

"Winning the championship means we accomplished the goal we set at the beginning of the season," said Al, Jr., "It means all the hard work and all the dedication, desire, and sacrifice that it takes to win the title is worth it."

Unser's intensity about and commitment to racing are well known. It has been said that if he had nothing to do but drive a race car, he would be behind the wheel 365 days a year.

Because racing is a total commitment of just about a person's whole life, Al, Jr., has had an advantage from belonging to a racing family. But

not all the family reinforcement is positive. "I've heard Al say that after he won the 1990 Indy-car series points championship, his dad and uncle told him, 'You ain't nothin' until you've won Indy,'" said Paul Tracy, the third driver on the 1994 Penske Indy 500 team. "And then he won Indy two years ago, and they said, 'You still ain't much—we've won it seven times.' That's a lot to live up to."

Al's racing style is said to be a combination of his uncle's and his father's styles. Bobby usually jumped out front in a race and stayed there. Al, Sr., usually waited around for 100 or 120 laps before he made his move.

Al, Jr., won four Indy car races in 1988, including this one at the Long Beach Grand Prix.

"Uncle Bobby was the kind of driver who could take a car that wasn't working very well and drive it a little out of control. He could do that and make the car go faster than it should," said Al, Jr. "I'm like Dad. If it doesn't come, it doesn't come. The car's got to be right."

Al Unser, Jr., won six races in 1988, two races in 1989, and six races and the season championship in 1990. But in 1991, 1992, and 1993 he won only one race in each year. According to one of his teammates, Al wanted a change.

Unser joined Team Penske at the end of 1993. He would race for Penske in the 1994 racing season, including at the Indianapolis 500.

Al, Jr., is married and has three children. Even his red-haired, six-year-old daughter Shannon was asked for her autograph after the 1994 Indy 500. Unser's other daughter, Cody, is eight. "Cody has already asked me if she can race go-karts," Al, Jr., commented. "I said she could as soon as she's nine. I'd be glad if all three of my kids ran at Indianapolis."

Twelve-year-old Alfred Richard (sometimes known as Mini Al, Just Al, or the new Little Al) Unser had his go-kart pulled for bringing home U's (for unsatisfactory) on his report card in 1993. "To see my son driving scares me to death," Al, Jr., said. "It gives me a whole bunch of different feelings I've never felt before. Something will happen to him and I'm shaken up, but he just laughs it off."

At the 1994 Indy 500, Al Unser, Jr., had a score to settle with teammate Emerson Fittipaldi. Sitting in the front yard of Al, Jr.'s home in Albuquerque is a section of wall from the Indianapolis Motor Speedway. The wall is a piece of the old turn 3, the spot Al, Jr., slammed into on the 198th lap of the 1989 Indy 500. Al, Jr., leading at the time, touched wheels with Fittipaldi and was knocked out of the race on the next-to-last lap.

"Fittipaldi used Al, Jr., as a wall," a friend commented. Fittipaldi sped on to win the race.

Unfortunately the 1994 Indy was turning out to be Fittipaldi's race too. Only 15 laps remained, and Fittipaldi had at least a 40-second lead, or almost a lap. The Brazilian driver shot his number-2 red-and-white Penske-Mercedes into lap 185 of the Indy track.

Just ahead of Emerson Fittipaldi, in car 31, was Al Unser, Jr. But Unser only looked like he was in the lead, since he was actually almost a full lap down. Fittipaldi had won the previous year's Indy 500 in addition to the 1989 one, and he had already run the fastest lap of this day's race: 220.680 miles per hour on lap 121.

"If we can lead this race without abusing the car, we'll do that," Al, Jr., remarked about his team before the race. "If we can't, we'll sit back and see what happens."

But from the beginning, Fittipaldi and Unser had easily outpaced the other cars with their new Penske-Mercedes engines. By the 13th lap Unser and Fittipaldi were lapping other cars. By the 38th lap only 16 cars were running on the lead lap; by the 57th lap only eight cars were. On the 70th lap Fittipaldi, Unser, and rookie Jacques Villeneuve had the lead lap to themselves. By lap 74 it was only the two Penske drivers. Paul Tracy, the third member of the Penske team, was out on lap 29 with engine trouble and would finish 23rd.

Fittipaldi led for 145 laps of the race and Unser for 48, putting the team in the lead for 193 of

Al pulls into the pits ahead of teammate Emerson Fittipaldi during a yellow flag at the 1994 Indianapolis 500.

the 200 laps total. Villeneuve, who would take second place with his Ford-Cosworth (an engine made in England by Cosworth for Ford), said simply, "I couldn't catch the Penskes."

But although the Penske cars had more horse-power—about 800, or as much as 200 horse-power more than the rest of the field—and handled better than the other cars, the race wasn't theirs for the taking. Al, Jr., had almost crashed during a rainy practice session before the race. "That scared me," he said. "When I went out to qualify, I had to build my confidence back up. If you've ever looked down a double-barreled shotgun, that was close to what it felt like."

Unser did get his car working well in the actual race. He had won the pole, or best starting position, with a qualifying speed of 228.011 miles per hour. But he was under no illusions that he had the race in the bag. "They say that on the last lap, you can hear every nut and bolt in your car. I was just wishing my Mercedes engine would keep running," he said.

The Andretti legend of horrors at Indianapolis continued when on lap 23 a $50 fuel-pressure-relief valve broke in Mario Andretti's car, putting him out of the race. Michael Andretti was penalized for passing a car while the track was under a yellow caution flag and took sixth.

Once the Mercedes cars had established their dominance in the 1994 Indy, another kind of race began. Even though Fittipaldi and Unser were teammates, driving for the same sponsors and owner, they fought for the lead against each other.

"On race day, Emerson is another car out there for me to pass to win the race," Unser said. "Once the green flag drops, he becomes the enemy."

On lap 185, Fittipaldi passed Unser in turn 1. Al, Jr., regained the lead on the backstretch. "Emmo was the strongest player," Unser said. "There were times when I went through a corner, my elbows were going crazy. I was getting sideways. I kept putting front wing [to produce downforce and improve traction] onto the car. Then with the last set of tires, the stagger went away."

Unser's radio had broken, and so he couldn't communicate with his pit crew. When he drove by the pit, they had to wave signs to tell him when he needed to stop for fuel and new tires. But with the radio out, no one could talk to him about racing strategy.

Suddenly Fittipaldi attempted to pass Unser once more. Although it looked like an unnecessary move, Fittipaldi really had to pass or risk losing the race.

The reason was Al, Jr., didn't need to make any more pit stops in the race, but Fittipaldi had to make one. Pit stops take a fairly long time, about 15 seconds if accidents don't happen, such as a crew member getting tangled up in a fuel line. The driver may also make a mistake at a pit stop. Even Unser, usually a master at pitting, had stalled out on one pit stop in the race, losing precious seconds. Race-car engines are prone to stalling coming out of the pit, because they function better at higher speeds—the turbocharger isn't making full power when they're idling or running slow.

But the real problem Fittipaldi faced with his last pit stop was that while he pitted, Al, Jr., would get even farther out in front of him. Although Al would still be most of a lap down, a wild card would remain in the race: yellow caution flags.

When danger exists on the track—for example, from a wreck or stalled car—the yellow caution flag is waved and the drivers must slow down and are not allowed to pass one another. But they are allowed to close the distance to the car ahead of them.

If there had been a yellow at the end of the 1994 Indy 500, after Fittipaldi had pitted for the last time, Al, Jr., could have come all the way around the track until his car's nose was right under Fittipaldi's tailpipe.

So Fittipaldi had a choice: 1) Don't pass Al, Jr., and hope there isn't a caution, or if there is, bet you can win a close race with Al right behind you; or 2) pass him as an insurance policy.

Fittipaldi went for the pass.

"You're not always thinking straight at the speeds those guys are going," said Owen Snyder. The long race might have taken its toll too: at the time of Fittipaldi's pass the drivers had been racing for over three hours, and they had sweated off six to eight pounds.

As Fittipaldi tried to pass, his car got caught in the turbulent air behind Unser's car. "The turbulence just washes out the front end when you get behind someone," Unser explained. "When he passed me, I had to get on the brakes hard and I barely made it. We came up on a lot of traffic and I was able to get back by him. He just went out too far and the old vacuum cleaner got him."

"I had everything under control," Fittipaldi said regretfully. "Then going into turn 4, I hit the apron. I just lost the back end. I was just about hitting the apron on every corner."

His car spun up across the track in turn 4 and smacked into the outer wall, then skidded in a fiery swirl down the main straightaway

Emerson Fittipaldi hits the wall trying to pass Al Unser, Jr. Fittipaldi had been a lap ahead, but Unser came back to win his second Indy 500 in 1994.

along the inner wall. The moment was almost an exact replay in reverse of Unser's crash in the 1992 Indy.

"I saw him hit the fence in my mirror," said Al, Jr. "I felt bad for him for about a second." But he understood why Fittipaldi had attempted to pass. "Here at Indianapolis, when you see a heavy hitter in front of you, you're going to do everything you can to put him a lap down. That would've put the final nail in my coffin."

Al, Jr., finished the 1994 race at a leisurely speed under a yellow caution flag after Stan Fox hit the wall on lap 196 and the debris was cleared.

And then Unser had won his second Indianapolis 500, at an average speed of 160.872 miles per hour, 15 miles per hour off the record average speed for the race. (Crashes and yellow caution flags had brought down the average speed.) The grueling race had lasted 3 hours, 6 minutes, and 29 seconds. Unser beat his average speed of 134.477 miles per hour in his 1992 Indy 500 win. And he took home $1,373,813.

Al, Jr., had just added another Indy 500 trophy to the eight the Unser racing family has already won, in the 28 years since Al, Jr.'s uncle Bobby won the Indy 500 in 1968.

After the race, Al, Jr., chugged the traditional bottle of milk given to the winner at the track. Then he and his father took a victory lap together in a pace car, the very car that Al, Sr., had won his last Indy 500 with in 1987, to celebrate Al, Sr.'s retirement and 55th birthday. Al, Jr., presented his victory to his father as a birthday present.

"This was neat. Real neat. I couldn't be happier and more emotional," Al, Sr., said later, leaning next to his motor home parked near the track.

But the victory scene wasn't entirely pleasant. Before, during, and after the race squawks of unfair play were heard about the Penske cars from other racing teams.

The wondrous Penske-Mercedes engines had been designed and built in England in just over six months. They were push-rod, similar to an ordinary car engine, instead of the overhead-cam the other Indy cars used. A loophole in the racing rules allowed push-rod engines about 20 percent more horsepower than the usual

Roger Penske notes his team has won 10 Indianapolis 500s. Al Unser, Sr., points out he has won four and Al, Jr., signals his two wins. Al Unser III has yet to win his first Indy. At left is the Borg-Warner Trophy, the official trophy of the Indianapolis 500.

overhead-cam type of race-car engine. The Mercedes engines had 55 inches of boost because of their push-rod design, while the rest of the field was allowed only 45 inches. The increased boost gave the Penske cars their horsepower advantage over the other cars in the Indy 500.

"They'll lose only if they screw up," said rival owner Derrick Walker of the Penske drivers before the race.

"They weren't even letting the cars all the way out," remarked Owen Snyder, team manager of Galles International Racing, which also ran a team against the Penske cars. "They were saving them."

Unser deserved credit for excellent, experienced driving in the race. He was no raw rookie at Indianapolis—he had won 20 races and almost $12 million in 13 seasons on the Indycar circuit before the 1994 Indy.

But no one disagreed that the Penske cars were the best at the race. Some said that only Roger Penske, with his finances and his determination to have an edge, could have successfully pulled off the Penske miracle at Indianapolis. "Roger Penske gets things done," Al, Sr., remarked.

"The Penske engine was just fine-tuning," said Bobby Unser. "Buick was building that same engine for probably 12 years without the success that Penske had; he just spent more money and made his a little better. Penske built the engine to the edge of the rules. Basically, real innovation isn't happening anymore in race-car design."

"We'll catch the Penske team," said Owen Snyder. "Galles had 17 wins with Al, Jr., from 1988 through 1993 against Penske's big bucks. Hard work does pay off."

In June 1994, the USAC changed the rules of racing so that the Penske cars couldn't have more than 52 inches of boost. Then in mid-August they limited the boost to 48 inches.

"This was politically motivated—no engineering data were collected before the change was made," Penske said angrily of the last restriction. In effect the 1994 Penske engines, with their 55 inches of boost, had to be totally redesigned for 1995. By 1996 the rule will be that all Indy cars have the same engine: a four-cam turbocharged racing engine with a 2.2-liter capacity. This is the same design the Ford-Cosworth and other engines currently running in Indy cars now have but half a liter smaller.

In the meantime, more Penske-Unser victories followed in 1994 in Milwaukee, Portland, Cleveland, and Lexington, Ohio, all races in the Indy-car series. Al, Jr., won those races after Indianapolis with an ordinary Ilmor/D engine—not the supercharged Penske-Mercedes V-8. He won the 1994 Indy-car series championship.

"I think at his age and experience, Al, Jr., has the potential to be a five-time winner at Indianapolis," said Roger Penske. "Rick Mears [another four-time winner] has said that." Five wins would set a record in the history of the Indianapolis Motor Speedway. With Al Unser, Jr., the Unser race-car legend seems sure to continue.

STATISTICS

Unser Wins at the Indianapolis 500

	Year	Starting Position	Average speed (mph)
Bobby Unser	1968	3	152.882
	1975	3	149.213
	1981	1	139.084
Al Unser, Sr.	1970	1	155.749
	1971	5	157.735
	1978	5	161.363
	1987	20	162.175
Al Unser, Jr.	1992	12	134.477
	1994	1	160.872

BOBBY UNSER: A CHRONOLOGY

1934	Born in Colorado Springs, Colorado, on February 20
1949	Starts racing stock cars in New Mexico
1950–51	Wins Southwest Modified Stock Car Championship both years
1952	Begins racing midget and sprint cars; wins three races
1953–55	Serves in U.S. Air Force in Albuquerque and races midget and sprint cars there and at Pike's Peak
1956	Wins championship car division at the Pike's Peak Hill climb, first win of what will eventually be a record 13 Pike's Peak titles
1963	Runs first Indy 500. An accident early in the race forces him out of the event
1967	Wins first Indy-car race at Mosport, Ontario, Canada. Sets a new track record; first win of 35 career Indy-car victories (fourth all-time)
1968	Wins first Indy 500 at record speed; first driver to run over 170 miles per hour at an Indy-car track. Wins United States Auto Club (USAC) National Driving Championship
1970	Places second to Al, Sr., in USAC standings
1972	Sets new qualifying mark at Indianapolis of 195.940 miles per hour; biggest leap in speed record in the history of the race. Fastest qualifier in eight of nine races run for the year, and led all nine races for a total of 520 laps. First driver to qualify at an average speed of over 200 mph (201.374)
1974	Captures second USAC National Driving Championship and named Martini & Rossi Driver of the Year. Wins first California 500
1975	Wins second Indy 500 and International Race of Champions (IROC) title
1979	Wins six races in Championship Auto Racing Teams (CART) Indy-car series
1980	Wins fourth California 500 (1974, 1976, 1979, 1980); only driver ever to win race four times
1981	Wins third Indy 500
1983	As car owner–team manager, wins Pike's Peak Hill climb with Al, Jr., driving
1986	Wins Pike's Peak Hill climb as driver in Audi Sport Quattro SL after 12-year absence from race
1987	Begins work as commentator for ABC Sports Television
1993	Wins inaugural Jaguar/Fastmasters Championship at Indianapolis Raceway Park. Sets new land-speed record of 223.709 at the Bonneville Salt Flats with a gas-powered modified roadster

AL UNSER, SR.:
A CHRONOLOGY

1939	Born in Albuquerque, New Mexico, on May 29
1957	First race in modified roadster in Albuquerque
1960	First Pike's Peak Hill climb—comes in second to brother Bobby
1964	Wins first Pike's Peak Hill climb, setting new course record and breaking Bobby's six-race winning streak.
1965	Wins second Pike's Peak. Drives in first Indy 500, finishing ninth
1967	Comes in second at Indy 500 to A. J. Foyt. Named Rookie of the Year in USAC stock cars
1969	Breaks leg in a motorcycle crash during his birthday party in Gasoline Alley the night before the Indy 500 and misses race
1970	Wins 10 of 18 races on USAC championship trial, including the Indy 500. Named Martini & Rossi Driver of the Year and USAC national champion
1971	Fourth (and last) driver to win two consecutive Indy 500s
1973	Wins USAC's dirt championship and Texas 200
1974	Finishes 0.5 second behind Bobby in the Ontario and California 500s
1976	Drives first Cosworth Ford–engine car ever to win an Indy-car race, the Pocono 500
1977	Wins first California 500; champion of the IROC series
1978	First to win the Triple Crown series of 500s: Indy, Pocono, and Ontario. Wins IROC series for second straight year
1983	Wins the Cleveland 500 and the CART/PPG Cup title with 10 top-five finishes in 13 races
1985	Co-drives with A. J. Foyt and others to win the Daytona 24-hour race. Wins CART/PPG Cup championship by one point over Al, Jr., with 11 top-10 finishes in 14 races. Leads Triple Crown drivers in points
1987	Wins fourth Indy 500, subbing for an injured driver, after starting 20th. Ties all-time record of 613 laps led at Indy
1991	Inducted into Motorsports Hall of Fame of America
1992	Finishes third in Indy 500, driving for the Menard Racing Team
1994	Retires from racing at Indianapolis 500, Memorial Day weekend, on his 55th birthday

AL UNSER, JR.:
A CHRONOLOGY

1962	Born in Albuquerque, New Mexico, on April 19
1978	Graduates from go-karts, dirt bikes, and snowmobiles to sprint cars. Travels southwestern sprint circuit
1979–80	Competes in World of Outlaws series. Meets future wife, Shelley, at Manzanita Speedway in Phoenix in 1980
1981	Wins Sports Car Club of America (SCCA) Super Vee title and Rookie of the Year honors
1982	Places fifth in Indy-car debut in the California 500 at Riverside International Raceway
1983	Youngest driver to pass the 200 mile-per-hour barrier at the Indianapolis Motor Speedway. First Pike's Peak win, setting record as youngest winner
1984	Wins first Indy-car race at Portland International Raceway on Father's Day
1985	Edged out for the CART/PPG championship by Al, Sr., by a single point, 151–150
1986	Finishes more races (14), completes more miles (3,782) and more laps (2,188) than any other driver en route to a fourth-place finish in the CART/PPG championship-point standings. At age 24, youngest IROC driver in the series history
1987	Wins second consecutive Daytona 24-hour race
1988	Joins Galles International Racing in Albuquerque. Records four Indy-car victories: at Long Beach, California; Toronto, Canada; the Meadowlands, New Jersey; and Miami, Florida. Wins second IROC title with victory at Watkins Glen
1990	Wins first CART/PPG championship, becoming first-ever second-generation Indy-car champion. Ties record for races won in a single season (six). Wins consecutive races at Toronto, Michigan, Denver, and Vancouver, establishing a CART record for victories in succession. Earns first Indy-car oval-track win at Milwaukee and first 500-mile win at Michigan in the fastest 500-mile auto race in history (average speed, 189.727 miles per hour)
1992	Wins first Indy 500 in closest race (by six feet) in Indy 500 history. With Al, Sr.'s victories, first time a father and son have won the race
1994	Joins the Penske racing team. Wins second Indy 500. More victories follow in the Toyota Grand Prix in Long Beach, California, Milwaukee, Portland, and Cleveland, all races in the Indy-car series; CART/PPG series points leader

FURTHER READING AND VIEWING

Indy 500 Video Series. Indianapolis: Indianapolis Motor Speedway, 1992, 1994.

Indy Review. Indianapolis: Indianapolis Motor Speedway, 1992, 1994.

Kirby, Gordon. *Unser: An American Family Portrait.* New York: Anlon Press, 1988.

Sullivan, George. *Racing Indy Cars.* New York: Dutton, 1992.

Weber, Bruce. *The Indianapolis 500.* Mankato, MN: Creative Education,1990.

ABOUT THE AUTHOR

Karen Bentley worked for Scientific American, Inc., and Random House–Knopf Children's Books in New York and has written three romances for young adults. She lives in Albuquerque, New Mexico, home of the famous Unsers.

INDEX

PICTURE CREDITS
Bob Tronolone, Burbank, CA: 2, 27, 34, 37, 47; AP/Wide World Photos: 8, 11, 45; Reuters/Bettmann:
12, 28, 50, 54, 56; courtesy of the Unser family: 15, 18, 20, 23, 24, 32, 43